T0198999

We Are the Trees

Marian S. Taylor

Illustrated by Amy Duarte

Balboa Press books may be ordered through booksellers or by contacting:

Balboa Press
A Division of Hay House
1663 Liberty Drive
Bloomington, IN 47403
www.balboapress.com
1 (877) 407-4847

Because of the dynamic nature of the Internet, any web addresses or links contained in this book may have changed since publication and may no longer be valid. The views expressed in this work are solely those of the author and do not necessarily reflect the views of the publisher, and the publisher hereby disclaims any responsibility for them.

Any people depicted in stock imagery provided by Getty Images are models, and such images are being used for illustrative purposes only. Certain stock imagery © Getty Images.

ISBN: 978-1-5043-7422-4 (sc)
978-1-5043-7423-1 (e)

Library of Congress Control Number: 2017901650

Print information available on the last page.

Balboa Press rev. date: 05/21/2020

BALBOA.PRESS
A DIVISION OF HAY HOUSE

We Are the Trees

Marian S. Taylor

Illustrated by Amy Duarte

As a little child I come to earth,
to learn the ways of the world.

I love all of nature, the sky, the trees
and the flowers, as petals uncurl…

Trees are an inspiration,
as they greet us every day.

They speak to us in the language of wind,
rustling as they sway…

I hear the trees singing gently
with each passing breeze,

"We are the trees, dear little one.
We are the trees."

I feel their beauty when the sun comes up
as they channel the light of the Divine.

Let there be Light… let the Light flow through…
Let it shine… Let it shine…

There are ancient traditions about carving masks and totems that reflect the Spirit of the tree.

There are artists with chainsaws and special tools
who shape and set the Spirit free.

Some trees keep my summer day cool
by providing welcome shade.

While some trees give up everything
to keep my winter fire ablaze.

Sometimes trees look like soldiers,
guarding the path along my way.

Sometimes they look like embracing lovers…
as with the wind they gently sway.

Towering over me… protecting me…
providing a peaceful place to play…

But bending and reshaping when workers cut branches
that seem to be blocking the way.

Each year as these trees grow older
and stand so straight and tall,

They provide new baby trees
as their many seeds so gently fall.

They stand so silently, caressing me
and sheltering me each step of the way.

These beautiful trees that guard my childhood,
as life's memories form deeper each day.

So, every time you near a tree and sense its wonderful spirit…
say a blessing…

And don't be afraid to give it a hug
and commune in this joyful caressing.

We are the trees, we are the trees...
providing shelter and sustenance and sharing our worth.

We are the trees, we are the trees... reaching to the heavens,
allowing light and life to reach into the earth.

We are the trees, we are the trees…

Be ever aware of our connection above
and receive Spirit's gift of peace and love.

Author: Marian S. Taylor

Marian S. Taylor, EdD, is a retired university professor. Her career began at the elementary level where she taught first grade and served as a reading specialist. She was director of the university laboratory school and a chairperson of a university department. She taught undergraduate and graduate classes while at the university and spent many years directing the program for the development of reading specialists.

Marian has been very involved with her family and with church activities. She is the mother of three grown children and is very proud of her grandchildren. Other publications can be viewed at www.marianstaylor.com

Illustrator: Amy Duarte

Amy Duarte began her career as an artist working for Walt Disney Animation Studios. From there, she leapt into the world of visual effects and graphic arts on more than 30 feature films like "Pirates of the Caribbean: At World's End," "The Amazing Spiderman," "Mr. and Mrs. Smith," etc. She was appointed as a lead artist for several major motion pictures, including "Fantastic Four," where she advised and guided a team of artists on creating the special effects of Jessica Alba's character (Sue Storm).

Born in Jakarta, Indonesia, and raised in three different countries, Amy is fluent in six languages and an avid polo player. She was also on the design team that created the top secret commercial for Apple's Watch before the product was launched. Her portfolio can be viewed at www.amyduarte.com.

Printed in the United States
By Bookmasters